A Metamorphosis Through Time

A Collection of Poems, Reflections, and Thoughts

Julia Kross

A Metamorphosis Through Time
Copyright © 2021 by Julia Kross

All rights reserved. No part of this publication may be reproduced,
distributed, or transmitted in any form or by any means, including
photocopying, recording, or other electronic or mechanical
methods, without the prior written permission of the author,
except in the case of brief quotations embodied in critical reviews
and certain other non-commercial uses permitted by copyright law.

Tellwell Talent
www.tellwell.ca

ISBN
978-0-2288-4817-2 (Paperback)
978-0-2288-4818-9 (eBook)

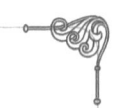

I dedicate this book to kindred spirits, whose life lessons have shaped the person they have come to be, as they continue to evolve on their soul's journey

Table of Contents

Part 1
Pain

Dark Shadow	3
A Pattern	4
Chaos	5
All it Takes	7
Alone	8
Why	10
I See	11
Sinking	12
Divided	13
This Brown Door	15
Drifter	16
Led Astray	17
Farewell	18
After the Fall	19
Never the Same	21
The 4 in me	22
A Private Conversation	23

Part 2
Love, Love Me Not

Heat	27
How	28
Crush	29
Acceptance	30
Taken	31
Twin Flame	33
If I Could	34
All I Wanted was You	35
A Memory	36

Broken	37
Spellbound	38
Race	39
Unrequited	41
Contact	42
Longing	43
If Only	44
Missing You	45
Frozen	46
Truth	47
Haunted	48

Part 3
Awake

Choices	53
Woman	54
Gaia	56
Angel without a Face	57
An Awakening	59
Celebration	60
August Sun	61
Ocean Star	63
Coming Home	64
A Message	66
My Only Love	67
One	69
Mirror	70
Recognition	71
Revealed	73
Soul Mate	74
I Remember	76

*Life is the spark of energy
that begins the journey
of our soul and Love
is what guides it*

PART 1

Pain

*Only the sea can still my mind,
while the sun warms my soul*

Dark Shadow

Darkness lives and breathes
in weak and strong.

Feeding on missing links,
it hides and lurks in shadows.

It waits…

waits for an invitation
but it doesn't just descend
unexpectedly.
It is born into all and given the
opportunity it –
        grows, grows, and grows like
        a child it plays, plays and plays

hide and seek.

And once this darkness matures
it knows no age, race, sex, or time.
It plunges into our minds and crushes
our spirit to the core, leaving us with nothing
but a dying soul.
Some open the door, give in
and sink
        deeper and
                deeper

into the void

while others only open the window,
breathe it in for a sparse moment until
they've had enough yet,

I remain

in its cell.

A Pattern

A sad child was she,
she wished it wasn't so
A tortured soul had she,
she wished she didn't know
While kids were playing
she was saying
why must people die?
While kids were laughing
she was suffering
And thus, her day would end
with a cry

Chaos

Obsessions, possessions
a stream of emotions
running away won't
solve the commotions.

Dreams and illusions
confuse my reality
taking me to a faraway place
of endless immortality.

Addictions, restrictions
a stream of contradictions
facing the facts won't
clear the convictions!

*When the mind is threatened by the heart,
it creates the illusion of fear*

All it Takes

One single thought –
    disrupts a peaceful night
    sneaks up beneath the twilight
    starts a moment of fear.

There's no one to share it with; there's no one here.

One single thought –
    begins a spark of insanity
    understands the reality of my mortality
    transcends beyond time and space.

The depths of my mind have much to face
Impossible to stop this quiet craze for
I have already leaped into a complex maze

One single thought –
    as my spirit escapes, my mind breaks…

                        is all it takes.

Alone

Lies, lies, and more lies
Is there no one out there to believe in?

Cries, cries, and more cries
Is there someone out there to confide in?

I wait. I crave for the moment to come
when I will free myself of this guilt.

I'm strong, I'm brave, at least to some
then why can't I break this wall I built?

They tell me I'm beautiful
I tell them they're mad

They tell me I'm wonderful
I tell them I'm sad.

More, more, no more, that's what I seek
Free, free, yes free, that's why I weep
cause I pray my soul to one day soar.

Is what I yearn for too much to ask?

So, here's to all who had faith in me
and tears to those who didn't believe in me.

When chaos is within us, it results from accumulated pain not yet healed. In turn, this chaos leads to a transformation that eventually leads to one's true path.

Why

Alone one stands in this time
Alone one's time is spent.

Alone one cries their pain on this passage
Alone this passage one takes.

Alone is what everyone shares
in common yet…separately.

So how is it that we feel the same?
Yet this does not comfort us

How is it that we ache the same?
Yet, this does not console us.

Why is it that one chooses to suffer
alone, when suffer do we all?

Why is it that one chooses to pretend
on their own, when pretend do we all?

One laughs among others
yet weeps among no one.

Why, why –
stand alone?

I See

As the bell tolls,
so does my mind
snap, snap,
snap
I left innocence behind
stop, stop,
stop
this madness

I wish to have my life back yet,
I know this cannot be
help, help,
help
my eyes saw
what they never
asked to see,
my heart felt what
it never intended to feel
I understand now, I do

The eyes, I blame it on

The **eyes**

Sinking

A thousand ships
have sunk my heart.
The ocean's current
was much too strong.

My love's sweet light
would never part
I thought this so
but I was wrong.

Locked away in
my own cocoon
I struggled with a
lonely possession

I looked for answers
on a full moon but
again – I drowned by
my own obsession.

Divided

Am I a simple girl living in a crazy world
who wishes to live a simple life?
That in itself is crazy
cause… let's face it
simplicity is hard to find.

Am I a crazy girl living in a simple world
who wishes to live a crazy life?
That in itself is simple
cause… let's face it
craziness is easy to find

so, what choose I?

Crazy and sane
or simple and insane?

What choose I?

What is destiny?

Is it choice or fate that determines one's path?

In making a choice, is that something we were fated to make? If so, can we change the choice we made? And in changing it, do we also change our destiny? Fate or Choice?

This Brown Door

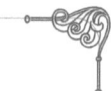

This brown door
stood long and strong
Twenty years lived behind it,
twenty years of
sleepless nights and
tormented dreams
This brown door
kept secrets well hidden
but not to those who
stood behind it
Love was no blanket
Time was an
enemy, it seemed
to never pass.
But what of those
lighthearted moments
where were they?
non-existent.
Yet even deep beneath
their blackened hearts
a day or two would shine
A short time lived however
for the haunting of
one sad soul would be
back to torment as before
And so, four souls sat
at a round table never
knowing when or why
destruction followed
This brown door
heavy with its burden
remained silent
in the night when
for one last summer
looked on its prisoners
no more

Drifter

He broods, he strides
He waits, he sighs
Unquenched is his thirst for life

He burns, he hates
He loves, he takes
Unsatisfied is his hunger for life

His mind is open
His soul is deep
His heart is kind
His secrets he must keep
Unshaken is his wall in life

His eyes tell all
His lips shall not
His smile shines bright
His silence says a lot

Unspoken is his past in life.

Led Astray

I fell upon a star one day
and not knowing why
I chose to stay

This star shone bright
and I for once had felt
not wishing for this
light to melt

But a fool was I to believe
this light for my opponent
had robbed me of my sight

So, I plunged in heart first
and reaped the glory
while my rival was working
to create another story

Then all my energy was
stripped away
and my soul fought not,

it went astray

Farewell

I see as deep
as winter snow
I know as much
as you're willing to show

A thousand pieces
I'm made to feel
for when I'm near
my heart you steal

My name's warm sound
whispered in my ear
sparks a million shock waves
and one single tear

So, forget me not
my sweet illusion
Hate me not
for my seclusion
Half a heart you
have for me

And love without passion
is where I don't want to be

After the Fall

A trance befalls me on my darkest day
as my limp body carries me to my bed
My heart tells me that all will be ok
but my mind disagrees with what my heart
has just said.

A corpse lies beneath my aching breast
as a silent whisper escapes my drying lips.
A weakened heartbeat echoes within my chest
reminding me of distant water that oh so
slowly drips.

Who am I, where am I
how did I get here?
Is it me, is it he or,
is it just plain fear?

My bed, my sleep
my eyes, oh how they weep
This mountain I must climb
seems way too steep

My passion, my life
myself, oh what strife
This pain I have shed
pierces sharper than a knife

My secrets, my lies
my heart, oh how it sighs
This moment I bear all
as my spirit before me dies

Nothing remains the same for too long, and nothing should be taken for granted

Never the Same

A wolf's cry slices
through the night

A bird's song disappears
at morning light

A distant voice I hear
calls my name

The voice that whispers
things will never

be the same

The 4 in me

My emotions like water run deep, they are immense and never-ending
My thoughts like waves change their course, they are wild and unconfined
My heart like a current takes me away, it pulls me down and lets me go
Calm and silent I am, but for a moment, strong and mutable I am, but for a moment
Magical and enchanting I am, but for a while, dark and unknown I am, but for a while
Who am I? you ask, I have but one answer, I am what you want me to be
I am your friend; I am your enemy

My emotions like air are a necessity to my existence, they are there but never seen
My thoughts like clouds are translucent, they are pure and, they are happy
My heart like an eagle soars high, it sweeps me up and brings me down
Fragile and sweet I am, but for a moment, thunderous and harsh I am, but for a moment
Warm and soft I am but for a while, cold and catastrophic I am, but for a while
Who am I? they ask, I have but one answer, I am what they know me to be
I am their friend; I am their enemy

My emotions like earth feel harsh, they are raw and ever present
My thoughts like a forest are vast, they are lost and they are scattered
My heart like a mountain runs steep, it is bold and, it is strong, or so it seems
Brittle and weak I am, but for a moment, dense and heavy I am, but for a moment
Dependable and grounded I am, but for a while, unpredictable and unstable I am, but for a while
Who am I? one asks I have but one answer, I am what one sees me to be
I am one's friend; I am one's enemy

My emotions like fire radiate an infinite heat, they are powerful and everlasting
My thoughts like the sun shed the light, they are inspiring and, they are bright
My heart like its rays penetrate through darkness, it pierces as it heals
Brave and untouchable I am, but for a moment, vengeful and blazing I am, but for a moment
Unstoppable and powerful I am but for a while, destructive and imposing I am, but for a while
Who am I? I ask, I have but one answer, I am what I was meant to be
I am my friend; I am my enemy

A Private Conversation

Ask not, want not
Is that what you ask of me
for am I free I ask of Thee

Yes, thou are free You say to me

But I do ask, and I do want
yet, You never answer me
So, what is it, that You ask of me
for what is free I ask of Thee

Free is Me You say to me

Then how do I become Thee
when me is who I want to be

Thou have always been Me
just ask yourself and will thyself to see
and you shall be

Search not, seek not, is that not
what You ask of me, for I was told
by others 'tis wrong to do so

To find truth wrong it is not
to abuse it, is You say to me

I understand Thee I do, but
free You have yet to explain to me

Free you are and always will be
that has not changed You say to me
Free you will be when thou love thyself
completely

Your perception of what free is needs
to be changed not Me, therefore
not thee

PART 2

Love, Love Me Not

*If love and paradise should be a flower,
then I would say it smells like oleander and jasmine*

Heat

scorches every surface of my skin

Yearning does every inch of me feel,
to satisfy this aching need

Restlessness begins to
take me,
sleepless nights threaten to
unhinge me

For no amount of water can
quench my thirst from this desire

Only the touch of a man, can cool my soul
and take me higher

How

Can one love without obsession?
Can one love without possession?
How does one love?

I seek a love that frees me
not a love that imprisons me

Can one love without restrictions?
Can one love without addictions?
How does one love?

I seek a love that releases me
not a love that suppresses me

Can one love without insecurities?
Can one love without worries?
How does one love?

I seek a love that encourages me
not a love that discourages me

Love in its purest form is what I seek
Love without perfection is what I need
Love that never dies is what I want

Love how bitter-sweet

Crush

Lips as red and
eyes as black
A handsome man
before me sat

Hair like night and
a voice to match
A restless soul
I cannot catch

He spoke to me and
I spoke back
A short time lived,
it couldn't last

Fire burned in my eyes
Shivers ran through my spine
A look, a flirt, a shame
His heart would never be mine

Acceptance

My soul saw recognition
for a fraction of a moment
It was the high I was looking for,
the sign I craved and then
my mind...
took control, to create fear,
to destroy me yet again

I have no one to blame but the depths
of my subconscious, that threatened
to steal my heart's content.

Taken

Hazel eyes see deep

        Hazel eyes seek truth

Eyes that see through the lies

        Eyes that know why love sighs

Your eyes, are my eyes

The past repeats itself to heal itself

Twin Flame

Will you let me be free
or cage me? For a caged
body bears me ill.

Will you allow my heart to sing
or crush it? For a crushed heart
bares me grief.

Will you nurture my spirit
or torture it? For a tortured
soul bears me death.

Leave if you wish to
enslave or possess me
stay only if you choose to
embrace and protect me
for I belong to no one but

Myself

Will I honour your strength
or fear it? For a fearing body
bears you ill.

Will I acknowledge your love
or destroy it? For a destructive
heart bares you grief.

Will I welcome your inner light
or darken it? For a darkened soul
bears you death.

I leave if I wish to
resent or demean you
I stay only if I choose to
trust and accept you
for you belong to no one but

Yourself

If I Could

force myself
to forget you I would
I'd convince myself
there's a reason why I should
But try as I may and
ignore as they say
my heart still wishes for
that single day
The day my maker will
unite my soul to yours
To embrace to touch to
feel your essence through
my pores

If I could force myself
to let you go I would
I'd deceive myself
into thinking that I could
But try as I may and
ignore as they say
my heart still wishes for
that single day
The day you will
look at me as one of
your kin
When you will at last
consider me as love's
sweet sin

If I could force myself
to love you no more I would
I'd subject myself to a life
I never understood
But try as I may and
ignore as they say
my heart still wishes for
that single day
The day my name is whispered
from your lips
In a heat of passion
where your hands
meet my hips

All I Wanted was You

Passing cars and changing lights
Busy streets bear lonely nights
Crossing paths was just a chance

Passersby and corner stores
Bus stop stands and closing doors
Crossing paths was no mistake

So, seasons change and
secrets grow
And memories remained of…
what no one will ever know

Now here I am in my bed
covers drawn up over my head

I tried to fight it
I lied to hide it
When all I wanted was you

You drove me crazy
My thoughts went hazy
Should I forget about you?

Now here I am on my own
once again by the phone

Fought to ignore it, craved to explore it
Truth be told all I wanted was you

Sought to destroy us, feared I'd expose us
Truth be told all I wanted was you.

A Memory

The smell of rain
moving through
deep green moss
reminds me of
what was mine

The air filled with
fear, of what once
took place long ago

It was dark and,
it was spring

A sword forged in
my heart with your
name which lingered
throughout time,
leaving me broken
and poisoned...

by a blade of silver
steel that robbed me,
of my love

Broken

They say a heart of stone
can never break
but I was wrong to test
the hands of fate

Our love grew stronger
through endless time
but my punishment bears
its unwanted crime

I failed you fair beloved but
not for what you think
My heart now missing us
like a chain without its

link

Spellbound

I cast a spell upon thee
that you shall want no other but me
Within lie the secrets that you seek
In binding you to me these secrets you shall keep
For if my magic is exposed to you
a curse shall fall upon thee
For he who knows will surely

                                fall

                                              into a hell

of eternity

Race

I will search for you no matter what,
wait for me my heart's desire

I will look upon your face once more,
wait for me my angel of fire

Look to me when all is in chaos
for I have been there from the start

I will stop at nothing to keep you safe,
no one and nothing can tear us apart.

A shooting star is seen, but for a split second, so does an opportunity that is never taken.

Unrequited

Love doubt the heart I sought,
I sought to make my own

Love capture the moment,
the moment I missed again

Love seek the man I want and,
to want the man that wants me

This love was never mine
and so, now love mends the heart that hurts,
it hurts as if for the first time

As time sows back my open wound,
love hopes that one day,

the day will come when I too,
will be the one for you.

Contact

A drop of rain
A blaze of heat
    A touch of pain
        Beneath my feet

A warm embrace
A soothing kiss
    A bed of lace
        A moment's bliss.

Longing

Light flickers across
the sea
in his eyes, I want
to be.

The moonlit light
sparkles in the dark
In his mind, I want
to embark.

Spring ends in the
month of May
In his heart, I long
to stay.

If Only

What would I do if I had the chance?
I would softly touch your lips
to feel love on my fingertips

What would I do If I went back?
I would hold you in a tight embrace
to feel your body as you caressed my face

What would I do If I had no fear?
I would straddle you where you lay
to feel your strength, it's where I'd stay.

If only it was so
If only…

Missing You

I long for you, my endless love,
even though we said goodbye

I'll never cease to wish to die
to have that single chance,

to see you in that special place
where once we forged our dance

The one of fire which sparked our soul
and now I'm left to fill that hole

Until such time I'll live my life
as though you were here by my side

I'll look for you, my eternal love,
while dwelling in the hands of fate

for I am not me without you nor
you without me, how long must I wait…

Here the one becomes two,
there the two shall be as one

Separate yet together are we
always remember, never forget

that my eyes once shut, I will
at last, be with thee.

Frozen

When I feel myself
slipping away, I remember
the magic of the moment
that left without a warning
never giving our love a chance.

Release me should you never
return for the pain still lingers
in between the loops of the invisible
chain that binds us, interlocked in a
universe that remains unchanged.

Truth

I don't want a man who needs to be mothered
there's only ever one of those beings,
the one who raised you

I don't want to control or tell you what to do,
that's for the insecure

I don't need to be treated like a queen,
I rule no kingdom except that of my heart

What I want is my equal, for only an equal
can bring the balance I seek in another

And although our bodies function differently
our souls are lit by the same fire
The burning light that is in you and me.

Haunted

Love, not be a flower to smell
for it will haunt me till tomorrow

Love, not be a person to hold
for I will miss it with great sorrow

*When darkness is penetrated by light,
it surrenders to its heat to transform into that
which it was destined to be...free*

PART 3

Awake

When fire burns all to ashes, what is left? Nothing
Yet, that nothing will one day turn into Something

Choices

My mother told me look for a heart
not a face for loyalty, not race
All that glitters isn't gold

My father told me look for love
not riches for sealed lips,
not one that snitches
All that glitters isn't gold

My brother told me look for
stability, not inconsistency
for protection and maturity
All that glitters isn't gold

Spirit told me look for me
for peace and ease of mind
not destruction, leave that all behind
All that glitters isn't gold

The stars inside me continue to
unfold.

Woman

Oh, how she walks with an air of mystery,
that no one can understand nor ever tried to

A smile hid the pain that she never showed,
only wrote about
Her heart searched for its truth
which she never ignored,
only listened to

Oh, how she walks with an air of unpredictability
which no one can guard against, nor even dared to

The eyes that told a story she never spoke of,
only wrote about
Her soul searched for its truth
which she never denied,
only lived by

The past, troubled but behind her
The present, awakened and within her
The future, unknown but in front of her

She is the Yin to her Yang

Fierce as a Lion

        Strong as a Bear

                Witty as a Fox

                        Fast as a Hare

Gaia

You call me mother but
you treat me like a stranger
an enemy you have conjured up
to justify your anger
You tested my patience
time and time again
yet I still allow you to be
I have shown you my power
yet you continue to ignore it
I have showered you with beauty yet
you choose to abuse it
How far will you go
How much will I take?

You call me mother but
you strip me
of my blood and my breath
a vengeance you've brought upon me
to ease your pain
I've tested your mortality
time and time again yet
you still insist on hurting me
I've shown you my wrath yet
you persist in mocking me
I've offered you my hospitality
but you continue taking advantage of it
How much can I take
How far can you go?

Our bond has weakened…
yes, a mother's love is
unconditional but the day
will come when I've had
enough and where once you came
from my flesh
I will send you back
as before where a new you
can emerge once more

Angel without a Face

Hidden in the curves of my mind
my soul stretched out for you,
not quite knowing who I was
aiming for

Still, I lay there waiting in my bed
hoping for that single voice
that would bring me out of
my self-made abyss

Buried in the depths of my core
my heart cried out for you,
not quite knowing who I was
calling for

Still, I lay there waiting in my bed
wishing for that single hand
that would heal my aching chest

Yet, somehow, in that moment of
feeling abandoned, a blanket of
the purest form descended on me.
A spark of electrical currents wrapped
around me and then –

a loving energy enveloped me
in its net holding me safely as
I slept

It was then I acknowledged it was you
You who never left my side,
who never judged nor, blamed

You who was there when I felt as if I died,
who took the hurt away which had me, chained

It was your hand that lay on my chest
It was your voice I heard in my mind

It was your strength that put my soul to rest
It was your love that I had asked to find
It was you, my faceless Angel

*Laugh said my mind; Live yelled
my soul; Love cried my heart*

An Awakening

A dream was it? Or was it real?
Felt like a dream
but it was my life
Unconscious I was for a while, a long
while. Like in my sleep of dreams
The earth was my bed
The trees were my walls
The passersby, my characters

A dream was it? Or was it real?
Felt like a dream
but it was my life
I thought this dream would end
only when I die and wake from
this trance called life
But see, my ego would have it so
not I. Unaware, it showered me
with lies to keep me asleep

No more.

I would soon emerge from my sleep
and open my weary eyes
as if for the first time
And so –
The earth is the ground I walk on
The trees are my friends
The passersby, my messengers
I alas have awoken from this endless sleep
to join my fellow man on a journey of
Now

Celebration

I envision myself
on the highest of cliffs
My only friend, the
ocean, surrounds me.
A tree of life stands on the edge,
underneath it, a table,
where one glass stays still
filled with rich red wine.
Music arises from within,
a warm breeze strokes
my face, sweeping through
strands of my hair,
as I begin to dance

I dance for love
I dance for beauty
I dance for life
I dance for me

August Sun

As I reflect on the silence that surrounds me,
no other sight has captured me so

For I long to feel its strength that
cannot be seen
I wish to smell its sweet scent that
cannot be tasted
I crave to embrace its warmth that
cannot be touched

To forever hold the light
that emanates from its soul

Look but don't touch, touch but don't feel, feel but don't fall, fall but don't love, said the mind.

Why asks the heart? I say look, touch, feel, fall, and love. Risk it all!

Ocean Star

Oh, wonders of the Sea
what lies beneath your bed?
Is it that which stirs within
our own soul within our head?
For the voice that is never heard
is your voice that echoes through
the waves of your world and straight
into the rays of our mind

I accept your intelligence
I acknowledge your frustration
I honour your spirit

Oh, wonders of the Sea
what corrupts your sacred space?
Is it that which crushes
our own humanity, our own race?
For the light that is never seen
is your light that shines through
the ocean's surface and straight
into the center of our heart

Oh, wonders of the Sea
My kinship to you will never cease,
for I am connected to you
and you to me

Coming Home

I searched for a place to call Home
I pleaded for others to show me the way
But the road ahead
let me find it on my own
What was I missing from life?
Why did I feel like a stray?

Broken hearts
Disappointing starts
Crushed hopes
Unclimbable slopes

I dreamed of this place called Home

I imagined a place to call Home
I called out for somebody to take me there
But my path ahead had led me to believe
I would make it on my own
What did I forget to look at?
What could I not see?

Determined steps
Unimaginable quests
Unfinished chapters
Unsolved matters

I dreamed of this place called Home

Only now I realize that I was in this place,
I so desperately looked for
It occupied an obvious space
yet well hidden in my core, it was in my center
It was the love I had stored for myself
to be given to me without judgment
The love that would never let me want for more

I am coming Home
I am remembering who I am
I have not forgotten
I am coming Home
I am honouring what I am

I am coming home to…

Me

By the sea, my love, it is there you shall find me

A Message

I seek you every night
while you watch over me
till morning light

I know of you and you of me
yet in my dreams, I want to see
your face, I cannot find
but for a tiny gleam within my mind

You chose to stay behind the veil
and let me go for one last time
But had I known what lay ahead
I'd never leave heaven's bed

Now here I am treading in lonely waters
till the day of my departure,
as you wait with endless certainty
for my exact arrival

You and I by the sea
basking in the sun's light
You and I for eternity
bound by a universal might

You and I by the sea
free as we will ever be
You and I by the sea
I'll meet you there
you'll know it's me

You and I together at last
moving forward
to seal our past

My Only Love

Love is yours; love is mine
Take my hand and realign
All is found when all is lost
I'll find you soon at any cost

Love is mine; love is yours
My heart awaits behind its doors
We merged as one long before
And now we merge forevermore

*Life was given, but the path
is yours to create*

One

From light to matter,
matter to light
From beginning to end,
end to beginning
The wheel of life burns as its spinning,
its flame intense and forever bright

It changes as it turns
yet remains the same
It houses many lessons
with only one goal to attain

From Source to being
being back to Source
The cycle of life holds our path,
a path that can never be forced

So be as you are,
an eternal shining star
and let your story unfold,
written, as it was long ago foretold

For it was you
who chose this road before you came
to learn at last that Me and you
have always been, One in the same.

Mirror

It is not in the colour of my eyes
nor in the shape of my lips
It is in the depth of my vision
and in the truth of my voice

It is not in the beauty of my skin
nor in the roundness of my breast
It is in the softness of my embrace
and in the kindness of my heart

So, look further than what the eye sees,
search deeper than the hand feels
and it is there you shall find peace

Friend, do not sway from reality
live not by illusion
For I am that which you are
I am your reflection
We all are

Recognition

And when he looked at
her and she at him
they knew

Her eyes were his eyes
looking back at her
and so…

His heart was hers

Forever

*An angel fell from grace to keep me safe and asked
for nothing in return, except my heart*

Revealed

Shattered glass reveals a secret
exposing me to your sight
Surrounded I am by your presence,
your eyes so still on this night

If I were to capture your essence
in a picture, I would touch it forever
If I were to capture this moment on film,
I would play it to no surrender

Shattered glass reveals many wounds
forcing me to remain open
Embraced I am by your boldness,
your strength remains unbroken

If ever I felt so weak yet so strong
It is now at this hour
If ever I felt so heavy yet so light
It is now within my power

Shattered glass reveals my fears
enabling me to deny you no more
Vulnerable I am to your knowledge
your heart penetrates like never before

Alas, I cry a sweet pain
releasing me of my past
For it is you my sweet rain
who has brought me here at last!

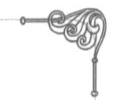

Soul Mate

Two Souls reunite
Two Spirits ignite
Free as the light they come from
Pure as the heart they connect from

Two Souls dance
Two Spirits romance
Graceful as a dolphin in the sea
In unison as the earth beneath its tree

Two Souls remember
Two Spirits surrender
Entwined as branches to a leaf
Eternal as the circle on a wreath

We can never all see through the same eyes so, focus on what the heart sees

Self-sabotage is not a solution, it's a crime committed towards you by you

Balance is key

Masks hide the truth so, wear none

I Remember

From sea to trees
and trees to sea
I am free…
I can run through a forest
or swim in an ocean
I could be what I want
I am free…
I could fly with my wings
to and fro in the sky
I can do what I want
I am free…

I know who I am now
two in one, I am fine now
I'm a fairy, a mermaid
I am neither nor the other
I am both, I am One
I am free…
I can sleep among lions
or play chase with dolphins
and can race with falcons
I am free...

Now that I embrace
and accept who I am,
will I be granted my true gift?
my reflection, my best friend
I am free…
From trees to sea
and sea to trees

I can finally see

Never doubt the heart for it is what will lead us to salvation
It is the light, the center, the vision, our treasure
It is the door to our soul, it is the truth
It is that which will free us from the shackles of our mind
Our body is its shelter, our eyes its window, so let us
look into this window and unlock the door to our Home

www.ingramcontent.com/pod-product-compliance
Lightning Source LLC
LaVergne TN
LVHW041649060526
838200LV00040B/1777